Nelson I

The Biography - From Prisoner to Freedom to South-African President; A Long, Difficult Walk out of Prison

By United Library

https://campsite.bio/unitedlibrary

Introduction

Nelson Mandela is one of the most inspiring and well-known figures in history.

This biography tells the story of his life, from being born into a royal family to becoming an anti-apartheid revolutionary leader and finally president of South Africa. It's an incredible journey that has impacted the world in immeasurable ways.

This book chronicles his life, from his childhood in apartheid South Africa to his election as the country's first black president. The book provides a detailed account of Mandela's trials and tribulations, as well as his eventual triumph over adversity. The book is an inspiring tale of one man's fight for justice and equality, and is sure to leave readers feeling inspired and hopeful.

You can learn about everything Nelson Mandela went through - the triumphs, the failures, and everything in between. This book provides an intimate look at one of history's most complex and fascinating figures.

Table of Contents

Nelson Mandela

Nelson Rolihlahla Mandela (July 18, 1918-Johannesburg, Gauteng; December 5, 2013) was a South African lawyer, *anti-apartheid* activist, politician and philanthropist who presided over the government of his country from 1994 to 1999. He was the first black president to head the executive branch, and the first to be elected by universal suffrage in his country. His government was dedicated to dismantling the social and political structure inherited from *apartheid by* combating institutionalized racism, poverty, social inequality and promoting social reconciliation. As an African nationalist and Marxist, he presided over the African National Congress (ANC) between 1991 and 1997, and at the international level he was secretary general of the Non-Aligned Movement between 1998 and 2002.

Originally from the Xhosa people and part of the Tembu royal house, Mandela studied law at the University of Fort Hare and the University of the Witwatersrand. While living in Johannesburg, he became involved in anti-colonialist politics, joining the ranks of the African National Congress and later founding its Youth League. After the National Party came to power in 1948, he gained prominence during the 1952 *Defiance Campaign* and was elected regional president of the African National Congress in the Transvaal province. He presided over the 1955 People's Congress. In his practice as a lawyer, he was arrested several times for seditious activities and, as part of the ANC leadership, was prosecuted in the *Treason Trial* from 1956 to 1961. Influenced by Marxism, he secretly joined the South African Communist Party (SACP) and served on its central committee. Although he favored non-violent protests, in association with the SACP he founded and commanded the guerrilla organization Umkhonto we Sizwe (MK) or "The Spear of the Nation" in 1961. In 1962 he was arrested and charged with conspiracy to overthrow the

5

government, for which he was sentenced to life imprisonment during the *Rivonia Trial*.

He was imprisoned for twenty-seven years, first on Robben Island and then in Pollsmoor and Victor Verster prisons. International campaigns advocated for his release, and he was released in 1990 in the midst of a social upheaval in South Africa. He intervened in political negotiations with Frederik de Klerk to abolish *apartheid* and set up the 1994 general elections, in which he led the ANC to victory at the polls.

During his Government of National Unity he invited other political parties to join his cabinet, and a new constitution was enacted. He created the Truth and Reconciliation Commission to investigate human rights violations committed during the *apartheid* years. Although he continued the liberal policies of previous governments, his administration implemented measures for land reform, the fight against poverty and the expansion of health services. At the international level, he was mediator between the governments of Libya and the United Kingdom in the trial for the bombing of Pan Am flight 103, and verified the military intervention in Lesotho. He declined to run for a second term in office, and was succeeded by Thabo Mbeki. After retiring from politics, he devoted himself to charity work and the fight against the AIDS pandemic through the Mandela Foundation.

In the words of van Engeland and Rudolph (2007), Mandela went from terrorist to politician to president of South Africa (1994-1999), making him a controversial figure for much of his life. His critics accused him of being a communist and a terrorist, although he won the support of the international community for his activism, which earned him more than 250 commendations and other awards, including the Nobel Peace Prize, the Presidential Medal of Freedom and the Lenin Peace Prize. In South

Africa he is loved and regarded as a figure of respect, where he is known by his native Xhosa clan name, *Madiba*, or *Tata* (father). He is also called the *Father of the* South African *Nation*.

Childhood

Nelson Mandela was born on July 18, 1918 in the village of Mvezo, located 53 km southwest of Mthatha, at that time part of the Cape Province.He was baptized *Rolihlahla*, a word of Xhosa origin meaning to *pull the branch of a tree* that could be interpreted as a *troublemaker*;although years later he would be known by his clan name, *Madiba*, after the death of his father he devoted much of his time to studies.A patrilineal ancestor - his great-grandfather Ngubengcuka - had been chief of the Tembu people in the Transkei territory, later part of the Eastern Cape. One of Ngubengcuka's sons, named *Mandela*, was Nelson's grandfather and the origin of his surname. *Mandela's* mother, whose only son he was, was originally from the Ixhiba clan and their offspring known as the *House of the Left Hand*. Although they were disqualified from inheriting the throne of Tembuland, they could succeed members of the royal council. Nelson's father, Gadla Henry Mphakanyiswa, was a tribal chief and advisor to the monarch of Tembuland; in fact, he had been elected to that position in 1915, as the previous one had been accused of corruption by a white official of the Union of South Africa.In 1926, Gadla was also dismissed when he was accused of corruption, but it is said that Nelson knew that he had lost his job by contradicting the provisions of this official.In addition Gadla was a polygamist, because he was a believer of the god Qamata,so he had four wives, four sons and nine daughters who lived in different locations. Nelson's mother was Nosekeni Fanny, a member of the Xhosa amaMpemvu clan, Gadla's third wife and a member of the lineage of the *House of the Right Hand*.

Mandela's early life was shaped, in his own words, by *custom, ritual and taboo*. He grew up with two sisters in his mother's *kraal in* Qunu where she tended cattle, so he spent a lot of time away from home with other boys his age. Although illiterate, his parents were devout Christians and so his mother sent him to a Methodist school when he was seven. Once baptized, he was given the English name *Nelson* by his teacher. When he was nine years old his father went to live in Qunu where he died of an undiagnosed illness, although years later Mandela would claim that it was a lung disease. This event made him feel *emancipated*, and he himself would affirm that from then on he inherited his father's *proud rebelliousness* and *obstinate sense of justice.*

By that time his mother took him to the palace of Mqhekezweni where he was placed under the guardianship of the regent Jongintaba Dalindyebo. He would not see his mother again for many years, but he came to consider that Jongintaba and his wife Noengland treated him as their own son, as they raised him together with their son Justice and daughter Nofamu. Since Mandela attended church services every Sunday together with his guardians, Christianity became an important part of his life. He also attended a Methodist mission located near the palace where he studied both English and Xhosa, as well as history and geography.From those years onwards, he became interested in African history, as he listened to the stories of the older visitors to the palace, and was also influenced by the anti-imperialist rhetoric of Chief Joyi, yet he regarded the European settlers as benefactors rather than oppressors. At the age of sixteen, Nelson - along with Justice and other young men - traveled to Tyhalarha to undergo the circumcision ritual that marked the transition from boy to man. Once completed, he was given the name *Dalibunga*.

Studies

Aiming to become a privy councilor to the royal house of thembu, Mandela started his secondary education in Engcobo at the Clarkebury Boarding High School which was a western education system, apart from being the largest school for black Africans in Tembuland, the egalitarian atmosphere of the school made him leave behind his aristocratic character, so he got to have for the first time a young girl among his friends; he also practiced sports and started his passion for gardening.After obtaining his certificate of studies of the first level of secondary school in two years, in 1937 he enrolled in Healdtown Comprehensive School, a Methodist institution in Fort Beaufort where most of the members of the royal house of Abu studied, among them Justice. The director of this school made prevailing the learning of the English culture and its system of government, but Mandela was more interested in the culture of the native peoples of Africa. He also befriended an individual who spoke the Sesotho language, so he was the first outside his Xhosa circle of friends; and one of his most favored teachers - of Xhosa origin - had married a Sotho woman, which was considered taboo. While he spent his free time in long-distance running and boxing, in his second year of school he acquired the rank of prefect.

Jongintaba also helped him to be one of 150 students who began studying for a B.A. degree at the University of Fort Hare, a prestigious black institution located in Alice, in the Eastern Cape Province, where he studied English Language, Anthropology, Politics, Native Peoples Administration and Roman-Dutch Law in his first year, with the intention of becoming an interpreter or clerk at the Department of Indigenous Affairs. There he studied English Language, Anthropology, Politics, Native Peoples Administration and Roman-Dutch Law legislation in his first year, with the intention of becoming an interpreter or clerk for the Department of Indian Affairs. He stayed in the Wesley House apartment building where he lived with K.D. Matanzima and Oliver Tambo, who would become his close ally for decades to come. As for extracurricular activities he took dance classes, and was part of a play about Abraham Lincoln, and also taught classes in a nearby community as part of the Student Christian Association.Although he had acquaintances who were associated with the African National Congress (ANC) and the anti-imperialist movement for an independent South Africa, Mandela avoided associating with them; in fact, he was a supporter of the British at the outbreak of World War II.On the other hand, he was involved in founding a committee that supported the interests of young freshmen who challenged the dominance of sophomores, and at the end of his first year he became involved in the Student Representative Council that protested the quality of food, for which he was temporarily suspended from the university. He eventually left the institution without achieving any degree.

In Johannesburg

When he returned to Mqhekezweni Palace in December 1940, Mandela learned that Jongintaba had arranged an arranged marriage for him and Justice, and to their surprise, the two decided to flee to Johannesburg by way of Queenstown. Surprised, the two decided to flee to Johannesburg by taking the Queenstown road, arriving in April 1941, where Mandela found work as a night watchman at the Crown Mines mining complex in what was his "first glimpse of capitalism in South Africa," but was fired when his boss discovered he was a fugitive.

While staying at a cousin's house in George Goch Township, he was introduced to real estate agent and ANC activist Walter Sisulu, who secured him a position as an apprentice in the law firm of Witkin, Sidelsky and Eidelman, headed by the liberal-minded Jewish firm of Lazar Sidelsky, to whom he was sympathetic in the ANC cause. The firm was headed by the liberal-minded Jew Lazar Sidelsky, who was sympathetic to the ANC cause. In this company, Mandela befriended Gaur Redebe, a young Xhosa member of the ANC and the South African Communist Party (SACP), and also Nat Bregman, a communist-minded Jew who became his first white friend.

Attending communist conferences and meetings, Mandela was impressed by the equal treatment of South Africans of European origin, Bantu Africans, Hindus and *Coloureds*. Years later he would state that he did not join the party because the atheistic positions of the organization conflicted with his Christian faith, and because he considered that the social conflicts in South Africa were essentially racist and not class struggle. Nevertheless, he became politically active and in August 1943 he took part in a successful boycott against the increase in bus fares. He also resumed his higher education, enrolling in a correspondence course at the University of South Africa, to which he devoted time in the evenings.

Mandela earned a modest salary, and was housed in a rented room owned by the Xhoma family in the town of Alexandra, which - though mired in poverty, crime and pollution - he considered a "nice place.He also began courting a young Swazi woman, although he was embarrassed to be short of money, before unsuccessfully courting the daughter of the owner of the place where he lived. He then decided to move to the Witwatersrand Native Workers Association compound where he lived with miners from various tribes. At the end of 1941 he received a visit from Jongintaba, who finally forgave him for his escape. When he returned to Tembuland in the winter of 1942, the regent had passed away, but he and Justice arrived the day after the funeral. By 1943, and when he passed his B.A. degree exams, Mandela returned to Johannesburg, Mandela returned to Johannesburg to become a lawyer, which would help him enter politics, an option he preferred to serving as a councilor in Tembuland, and years later he would say that it was not an emotional decision, but that in reality "I wanted to do it, and it could not be otherwise.

Law Studies and the ANC Junior League

When he began his law studies at the University of the Witwatersrand, Mandela was the only black student and - although he suffered racial discrimination - he was able to make a variety of friends among liberal and communist-minded Europeans, as well as Jews and Hindus, including Joe Slovo, Harry Schwarz and Ruth First.By the time he joined the ranks of the ANC, Sisulu was very influential himself and spent much of his time with other activists at Sisulu's own home in Orlando in the Soweto urban area, including Oliver Tambo.By 1943, he met Anton Lembede, an African nationalist who was opposed to any heterogeneous front against colonialism and imperialism, and also to an alliance with the communists. Although Mandela was against this position (as he had friends of various races, including communists), he supported Lembede, believing that black Africans should be independent in their struggle for political self-determination.Also, endorsing the need for a youth front to counter oppression, he was part of a delegation that approached ANC President Alfred Bitini Xuma at his Sophiatown dwelling house. This was the origin of the African National Congress Youth League (ANCYL) on Easter Sunday 1944 at the Bantu Men's Social Center on Eloff Street, Lembede having been appointed chairman, while Mandela was a member of the executive committee.

At the Sisulu home, Mandela met Evelyn Mase, an ANC activist from Engcobo who was training to become a nurse. The two married in October 1944 and - after living at her parents' home - rented house no. 8115 in Orlando in early 1946. The couple's first child, Madiba *Thembi* Thembekile, was born in February 1945, followed by their daughter Mazawike in 1947, who died nine months later of meningitis.Mandela enjoyed his home life which was joined by his mother and sister Leabie at his request. In early 1947 the three-year apprenticeship ended at the firm of Witkin, Sidelsky and Eidelman, so he devoted himself full time to his studies, while supporting himself on loans from the Bantu Welfare Trust.

In July 1947 Mandela had to rush Lembede to a hospital, where he died. Lembede was succeeded as president of the ANCYL by Peter Mda, a moderate, who agreed to cooperate with communists and activists of other races. On assuming the post he appointed Mandela as his secretary.However, Mandela would come into disagreement with Mda when in the month of December 1947 he supported the expulsion of communists from the ANCYL on the grounds that their ideology was incompatible with Africans, although this action was unsuccessful.That same year he was elected to the ANC executive committee in Transvaal, under the leadership of regional chairman C.S. Ramohanoe; who subsequently acted against the interests of the regional committee by associating with Hindus and communists. In the end Ramohanoe resigned and Mandela is said to have had much influence in his resignation.

For the South African general elections of 1948, in which only white citizens voted, the Herenigde Nasionale Party - controlled by Afrikaners and headed by Daniel François Malan - took power, and together with the Afrikaner Party formed the National Party, a political institution that was openly racist and promoted the legalization of segregation with new apartheid regulations. This political institution was openly racist and promoted the legalization of segregation with the new apartheid regulations. By that time Mandela was gaining influence in the ANC and together with his supporters began to take actions against apartheid, which consisted of boycotts and strikes, strategies taken from the Hindu community residing in South Africa. The president of the ANC, Alfred Bitini Xuma, did not support these measures, so he was removed from office and replaced by James Moroka, who was backed by an extremist board that included Sisulu, Mda, Tambo and Godfrey Pitje. Mandela himself would assert that at that time they had led the ANC "down a more radical and revolutionary path" and, because he had his time occupied with politics, Mandela was unable to complete his final year at the University of the Witwatersrand and was denied his degree in December 1949.

The Challenge Campaign and the ANC presidency in the Transvaal.

The seat left by Xuma on the ANC national executive committee was taken by Mandela in March 1950.That same month, the Convention for the Defense of Freedom of Expression took place in Johannesburg, attended by Africans, Hindus and communists, who called for a general strike against apartheid. Mandela opposed this because it was not led by the ANC; despite this, many black workers took part in it, which caused police repression and the entry into force of the Suppression of Communism Act, which affected the activity of the agitators.That year he was also elected president of the ANCYL. For the national conference in December 1951, he continued to oppose the formation of a heterogeneous front of struggle, but his position was outvoted.Therefore, he changed his point of view and adhered to this decision. Moreover - under the influence of his friends, among them Moses Kotane, and due to the support given by the Soviet Union to provoke wars of independence - his distrust of communism was put aside. As a result he became interested in the texts of Karl Marx, Friedrich Engels, Vladimir Lenin, Joseph Stalin and Mao Zedong, and ended up adopting dialectical materialism.By April 1952 he began working with the law firm of H. M. Basner, which - together with his growing political activism - meant that he spent less time with his family.

In the same year, the ANC began to prepare the *Campaign for the Defiance of Unjust Laws* together with Hindus and communist-affiliated groups, and a board was set up to recruit volunteers. The organization decided on a policy of nonviolent resistance, inspired by Mahatma Gandhi. There were those who considered this an "ethical" choice, while Mandela considered it a "pragmatic" choice.By June 22, during a demonstration in Durban,

Mandela delivered a speech to 10,000 people that was the start of the protests and also led to his arrest, for which he was briefly incarcerated in Marshall Square Prison.With the campaign underway, ANC supporters increased from 20,000 to 100,000. For its part, the government responded with mass arrests and would enact the Public Safety Act for the following year, which ushered in martial law.By May, the authorities prevented the ANC's Transvaal regional chairman, John Beaver Marks, from making public appearances; in response, Marks recommended Mandela as his successor. Although the radical Bafabegiya group opposed his candidacy, he was elected to the post in October.

On July 30, 1952, Mandela was arrested under the legal provisions of the Suppression of Communism Act and brought to trial in Johannesburg along with 21 other defendants, among them Moroka, Sisulu and Yusuf Dadoo. All were found guilty, but the nine-month sentence of hard labor ended up suspended for two years.By December, Mandela was banned for six months from attending public meetings or conversing with more than one person, which caused his chairmanship of the ANC in the Transvaal region to become unviable. By this time, the *Defiance Campaign* had waned.In September 1953, Andrew Kunene read on his behalf the speech *The Long Road to Freedom* at an ANC meeting in Transvaal, the title of which was taken from a quote by the Hindu independence leader Jawaharlal Nehru, a major influence on Mandela's thinking. The speech laid the groundwork for a possible plan in case the ANC was declared illegal. This plan, also called *M-Plan*, provided for the division of the organization into cells with a centralized leadership.

On the other hand, once he passed the exams required to practice law, Mandela was able to secure a position with the firm of Terblanche and Briggish, before switching to Helman and Michel, whose managers were liberal-minded, and by August 1953, he and Oliver Tambo founded their own firm, which was domiciled in downtown Johannesburg. In fact, it was the only one run by black professionals in the entire country, and was in great demand by clients outraged by police brutality. However, the firm was not well received by local authorities, so it was forced to move to a remote location when its legal permit was withdrawn on the basis of the Group Areas Act. To make matters worse - and despite the birth of their second daughter, Makaziwe Phumia, born in May 1954 - Mandela's relationship with Evelyn deteriorated to the point that she accused him of adultery. Years later it would be proven that he had had a relationship with ANC member Lillian Ngoyi and secretary Ruth Mompati with whom he is said to have fathered a child, a fact that has not been proven. Disgusted by her son's behavior, Nosekeni Fanny returned to Transkei, while Evelyn, equally annoyed by Mandela's political activity, became a follower of the Jehovah's Witnesses.

The People's Congress and the Treason Trial

Mandela had come to the conclusion that the ANC "had no alternative but armed resistance" after taking part in a failed protest in February 1955 against the demolition of Sophiatown, a Johannesburg suburb populated entirely by black families, and recommended to Sisulu that he request armaments from the government of the People's Republic of China, which - although it supported the anti-apartheid movement - believed they were not sufficiently prepared for a guerrilla war. By that time - together with the South African Indian Congress, the Congress of Citizens of Mixed Origin, the Congress of Trade Unionists and the South African Congress of Democrats - the ANC prepared the 1955 People's Congress, which called on all South Africans to submit proposals for a post-apartheid era. Based on the responses, a Freedom Charter was written by Rusty Bernstein calling for the creation of a democratic and non-racist state, plus the nationalization of industry. The document was accepted in June 1955 at a conference in Kliptown attended by 3,000 delegates, but was broken up by the police. Despite this, the significance of the event remained in Mandela's mind.

At the end of another period of legal restriction on his person in September 1955, Mandela went to the Transkei to discuss the implications of the Bantu Authorities Act with tribal leaders, and took the opportunity to visit his mother and Noengland before traveling to Cape Town. In March 1956 he received his third court ban from appearing in public, which prevented him from moving out of Johannesburg for five years, although he always found ways to circumvent the order. Moreover, his marital relationship came to an end, so his wife Evelyn took their children to live with her brother. The divorce process began in May 1956, in which she alleged physical abuse on her person by Mandela who denied the charges, apart from the fact that he demanded custody of the children. Although she withdrew the lawsuit in November, Mandela restarted the process in January 1958 and two months later the divorce decree was decreed that put the custody of the children in charge of Evelyn.While the trial was developing, Nelson began to relate with the social worker Winnie Madikizela, with whom he married in Bizana on June 14, 1958. She would become involved in ANC activities, which led to his imprisonment on more than one occasion.

On December 5, 1956, Mandela was arrested along with most of the ANC executive committee for "high treason" against the state. The trial was held in Johannesburg prison amid popular protests, with the defendants undergoing a preliminary examination hearing on December 19 at Drill Hall, before being released on bail.Arguments by the defense began on January 9, 1957. Led by attorney Vernon Berrangé, the litigation continued until it was adjourned in September. In January 1958, Justice Oswald Pirow was chosen to try the case, and in February he decreed that there was sufficient evidence for the trial to be taken up by the Transvaal High Court.The formal trial of the so-called *Treason Trial* began in the city of Pretoria in August 1958, in which the defenders succeeded in having the three judges - all of whom were linked to the National Party - replaced. One of the charges was dismissed and by October the accusers changed the accusation, and restated the version that the ANC leaders had committed high treason and called for a violent revolution, a charge refuted by the defenders.

By April 1959, a faction of militants dissatisfied with ANC policy decided to found the Pan-African Congress (PAC), having elected Robert Sobukwe as its president, and Mandela - a friend of Sobukwe's - was of the opinion that the members of this organization were inexperienced.

Mandela - Sobukwe's friend - was of the opinion that the members of this organization were inexperienced. In spite of this, both the PAC and the ANC carried out a campaign in May 1960, in which they burned the passes that black Africans were obliged to carry. One of the protests, organized by the PAC, was repelled by the police and resulted in the deaths of 69 agitators in what would become known as the Sharpeville Massacre. As a show of solidarity, Mandela publicly burned his own pass as a riot broke out across South Africa, prompting the government to issue martial law.Under this state of emergency, Mandela and other activists were arrested on March 30 without charge and confined in the dilapidated and filthy Pretoria prison, while the ANC and PAC were outlawed. The prisoners' lawyers found it difficult to see them, prompting the *Treason Trial* team to withdraw from the trial in protest. However, the defendants defended themselves and were released when the state of emergency was lifted at the end of August. Mandela then took it upon himself to organize the Pan-African Conference near Pietermaritzburg, Natal Province, in March, which was attended by 1,400 anti-apartheid delegates and agreed to shut down the country on May 31, the day South Africa became a republic.By March 29, 1961, after six years of court litigation, the judges issued the sentence in which they found the accused not guilty, which left the government's actions in question.

MK and the South African Communist Party

Disguised as a chauffeur, Mandela traveled across the country organizing a new ANC political cell and a mass strike for the last days of May 1961. At the time he was known as the "black pimpernel" in the country's press, an allusion to the character in Emma Orczy's 1905 novel *The Scarlet Pimpernel. However,* the police had already issued a warrant for his arrest, yet he held secret meetings with the same reporters, and after the government had failed to break the strike, he himself warned that many anti-apartheid activists would resort to violence, including the radical *Poqo* faction, the military wing of the PAC. In fact, he believed that the ANC should form its own armed group, so he convinced other allied groups and ANC leader Albert Lutuli, who was opposed to any violent action, of this radical step.

Inspired by Fidel Castro's 26th of July Movement, in 1961 Mandela co-founded Umkhonto we Sizwe (*The Spear of the Nation,* also known by the acronym MK), together with SACP leader Joe Slovo and also Walter Sisulu. As the leader of the group, he began to learn from clandestine literature on guerrilla warfare by authors such as Mao Zedong and Ernesto "Che" Guevara. Although the organization was born separate from the ANC, in later years MK became its armed wing. Among the original members were white communists, and after hiding in the apartment of communist Wolfie Kodesh in Berea, Mandela moved to Liliesleaf Farm in Rivonia where he met with Raymond Mhlaba, Joe Slovo and Rusty Bernstein who wrote MK's constitution.

For its part, and through the organization of cells, MK agreed to carry out sabotage actions, although seeking the minimum of casualties to put pressure on the government.

The operations would include explosions in military installations, nuclear plants, telephone lines and road systems, which would be carried out at night to avoid crowds. Mandela himself asserted that they had chosen sabotage not only because it was the option that caused the least amount of damage, but because "avoiding loss of life was the best way to seek reconciliation between the different races in the years to come". It also noted that there were "strict orders to MK members to avoid loss of life," although if this failed, MK would resort to "guerrilla warfare and terrorism." Following the news that Albert Lutuli had been awarded the Nobel Peace Prize, MK proclaimed its existence and announced the explosion of 57 bombs on the Oath Day holiday (December 16, 1961), followed by other ambushes on the last day of the year.

At that time, the ANC arranged to send Mandela as a delegate to the Pan-African Meeting for the Freedom of East, Central and Southern Africa (PAFMECSA) in February 1962, which was to take place in Addis Ababa (Ethiopia). He made the trip in secret, but managed to meet Emperor Haile Selassie I in front of whom he delivered a speech at the meeting.Later he went to Cairo, Egypt, where he admired the political reforms of President Gamal Abdel Nasser, and then he went to Tunis where President Habib Bourguiba donated him 5000 pounds sterling to buy weapons. He continued his tour in Morocco, Mali, Sierra Leone and Senegal, and received money from Presidents William Tubman of Liberia and Ahmed Sékou Touré of Guinea. On his way to London, he met other anti-apartheid activists, as well as journalists and well-known left-wing politicians. When he returned to Ethiopia, he started a six-month guerrilla warfare course, of which he completed only two months when he was asked to return to South Africa.

Arrest and the Rivonia Trial

On August 5, 1962, the police captured Mandela and Cecil Williams near Howick. Several people have been suspected of having informed the police of Mandela's whereabouts, among them journalist G.R. Naidoo, white individuals from the South African Communist Party and the CIA itself, although Mandela never considered these claims credible and instead attributed his arrest to his own carelessness.About the CIA, Mandela's official biographer, Anthony Sampson, has maintained that this conjecture "was unfounded". Once imprisoned in Johannesburg at Marshall Square Prison, he was accused of inciting a workers' strike and leaving the country without permission. He defended himself and chose Slovo as his legal assistant, and intended to use the trial as a form of "ANC moral opposition to racism". He also had demonstrations of support for himself outside the courthouse premises.Upon his transfer to Pretoria, where Winnie managed to visit him, he began correspondence studies for a law degree from the University of London.The initial hearing was held on October 15, which was disrupted by Mandela's decision to wear traditional *Kaross* attire; he also refused to call witnesses and was given the task of changing his pleadings into a political speech. At the end of the trial he was found guilty and sentenced to five years in prison. Meanwhile, as he left the courtroom his supporters sang the *Nkosi Sikelel' iAfrika* anthem.

On July 11, 1963, the police raided the Liliesleaf farm where they proceeded to arrest its occupants and confiscated paperwork related to the activities of the MK, where in certain documents Mandela was mentioned. This investigation was the origin of the *Rivonia Trial* that took place in the Pretoria High Court from October 9, in which Mandela - already imprisoned and together with other supporters - was charged with four counts of sabotage and conspiracy to overthrow the government. His main accuser was Percy Yutar, who requested the death penalty for the accused. Judge Quartus de Wet dismissed the claims due to insufficient evidence, but Yutar changed the accusations and presented new evidence between December 1963 and February 1964, a period in which 173 witnesses were called, as well as abundant documented and photographic evidence was presented.Before the court he delivered his last speech in freedom where he said: "I have always treasured the ideal of a free and democratic society in which people can live together in harmony and with equal opportunities. It is an ideal for which I have lived. It is an ideal for which I hope to live, and if necessary, it is an ideal for which I am willing to die."

With the exception of James Kantor, who was found not guilty on all charges, Mandela and the other defendants admitted sabotage but denied that they had intended to launch a guerrilla war against the government. In fact, at the trial they emphasized their political activity. At the beginning of the defense arguments, Mandela delivered a three-hour speech (known by the title *I am prepared to die*), inspired by Fidel Castro's own *History will absolve me*. This plea was broadcast in the print media despite official censorship, and has been recognized as one of his best speeches. The trial drew the attention of the international community, and there were calls for the release of the defendants from institutions such as the United Nations and the World Peace Council. In London, students at University College elected Mandela as their honorary president, and vigils were held in his honor at St. Paul's Cathedral.In contrast, the South African government regarded Mandela and his supporters as violent saboteurs with communist ideas, and on June 12, 1964, Judge Quartus de Wet found Mandela and two of his accomplices guilty on all four counts and sentenced them to life imprisonment.

Prisoner on Robben Island

Mandela and the other convicts were transferred from Pretoria to the prison on Robben Island, where they would remain for eighteen years. He was held separately from the common prisoners in *section B*, and was confined in a damp cell 2.4 m high by 2.1 m wide with a palm mat for sleeping.The *Rivonia Process* prisoners worked at crushing stone for gravel, and were constantly harassed by verbal insults and physical assaults from the all-white guards until they were transferred to a lime mine. At first Mandela was not allowed to wear sunglasses, so the glare from the lime damaged his visibility. At night he continued his law studies, but was forbidden to read newspapers and on several occasions was punished with solitary confinement for possessing news clippings. In fact, he was classified as a *class D* prisoner, the lowest grade in the prison and was allowed to receive one visit and one letter every six months, although mail was under censorship.

However, political prisoners took part in hunger strikes to improve prison conditions, in what was seen as a way to continue the anti-apartheid struggle, even though Mandela considered it futile.In addition, the prisoners belonging to the ANC elected Mandela, Sisulu, Govan Mbeki and Raymond Mhlaba as a kind of "commission of notables", and Mandela himself became part of a group representing all political prisoners on the island, thus establishing communication with members of the PAC and the Yu Chi Chan Club.He also took part in what was called the "Robben Island University" where the prisoners made known their own points of view of their field of knowledge, apart from debating topics such as homosexuality and politics, the latter which led to intense discussions with Marxists, among them Mbeki and Harry Gwala.On the other hand, he attended Christian Sunday schools where he learned about Islam and also studied the Afrikaans language, which he hoped would foster mutual respect with the guards and attract them to his cause.

Despite his imprisonment, Mandela was visited by well-known South African personalities, the most important of whom was parliamentary representative Helen Suzman of the Progressive Party, who supported his cause outside prison. The most important of these was parliamentary representative Helen Suzman of the Progressive Party, who supported his cause outside prison.In September 1970 he met with Dennis Healey, a member of the British parliament and part of the Labour Party.South Africa's Minister of Justice, Jimmy Kruger, visited him in December 1974, but the two did not seem to hit it off.His mother visited him in 1968 but died soon after, and his first-born son *Thembi* died in a car accident the following year.However, he was not allowed to attend the funerals of both of them. However, he was not allowed to attend the funerals of both.His wife was allowed to visit him on occasion, although she fell into prison regularly for her political activity; and his daughters saw him for the first time in December 1975. Winnie was released from prison in 1977 but was forced to take up residence in Brandfort, which prevented her from visiting him.

From 1967 prison conditions improved. Black prisoners were allowed to wear long pants instead of shorts; they were allowed to engage in recreational activities and the quality of food was improved, and Mandela later commented that soccer had made them "feel full of life and very cheerful despite their situation.

By 1969 an escape plan was hatched for Mandela by his friend Gordon Bruce, but it was discarded because they had been infiltrated by an agent of the Office of State Security, who intended to have Mandela shot during the escape.By 1970 Commandant Piet Badenhorst took control of the prison, which increased the physical and verbal abuse, but Mandela complained to visiting judicial authorities and Badenhorst was eventually transferred and replaced by Commandant Willie Willemse who fostered a fruitful relationship with Mandela, and was keen to further improve conditions in the prison.

By 1975 Mandela was already considered a *class A* prisoner, which allowed him to have many visitors, including Mangosuthu Buthelezi and Desmond Tutu, and he also received regular correspondence. That year, he began writing his autobiography, which he secretly sent to London, although it remained unpublished for several years. However, prison authorities found several pages written, which caused his study privileges to be suspended for four years, and he devoted his free time to gardening and reading until he resumed his studies for a law degree in 1980.

By the late 1960s, Mandela's fame had been overshadowed by Steve Biko and the Black Consciousness Movement (BCM). The BCM considered the ANC ineffective, so it called for active militancy, although after the 1976 Soweto riots many BCM supporters ended up imprisoned on Robben Island. Mandela tried to relate to these radical-minded young people, even though he was highly critical of their positions and their antipathy to white anti-apartheid activists.By the time he was 60 years old, the international community's interest in his situation was restored, and he was awarded an honorary doctorate in Lesotho, India's Jawaharlal Nehru Award in 1979, and the *Keys to the City of* Glasgow, Scotland, in 1981.By March 1980 the slogan "Free Mandela!" was launched by journalist Percy Qoboza, prompting an international campaign led by the United Nations Security Council for his release. Despite this international pressure, the government refused to release him and sought the support of its allies, including U.S.

President Ronald Reagan and British Prime Minister Margaret Thatcher, who supported the ANC's removal.

At Pollsmoor Prison

In April 1982, Mandela was transferred to Pollsmoor Prison in Tokai, a suburb of Cape Town, along with Walter Sisulu, Andrew Mlangeni, Ahmed Kathrada and Raymond Mhlaba, who believed they were being isolated to avoid influencing the younger prisoners. Conditions at Pollsmoor were better than on Robben Island, although Mandela missed the companionship and the natural space around the island. He also hit it off with Pollsmoor's warden, Brigadier Munro, who allowed him to organize a roof garden and increased his reading and mailing, as he was allowed to dispatch 52 letters a year. At Pollsmoor he was elected as the godfather of the multiracial United Democratic Front (UDF), which was founded to combat the 1983 reforms to the South African constitution implemented by President Pieter Willem Botha. In these reforms, the National Party had allowed *Coloureds* and Hindus to vote to elect their own parliaments, who could legislate on education, health and housing, but black Africans were excluded from this new regime. The UDF and Mandela shared the view that such reforms were a way of dividing the anti-apartheid movement.

By this time, violence in South Africa had escalated, leading many to fear civil war. In fact, under international pressure, multinational banks stopped investing in the country, which caused the economy to slow down. These same entities, and personalities such as Margaret Thatcher who had already changed her position,[*citation needed*] urged for the release of Mandela, who was at the height of his fame around the world, in order to ease the tense political situation. Although he was considered a "recalcitrant Marxist", in February 1985 President Botha offered his release on the condition that he "unconditionally rejected violence as a political option". Mandela refused the proposal, and made his position known through his daughter Zindzi in which he stated "What freedom are you offering me while the ANC is outlawed? Only free men can negotiate. A prisoner cannot."

In 1985 he underwent surgery for an enlarged prostate, before being transferred to a cell on the second floor, where he held meetings with seven personalities who made up an international delegation trying to establish negotiations with the government, but Botha refused to cooperate; in fact, in June he declared a state of emergency and deployed police to subdue any revolt. The anti-apartheid movement responded to the government's actions: the ANC committed 231 sabotages in 1986, and 235 in 1987. Using armed force and right-wing paramilitaries to combat the resistance, the government secretly sponsored the Zulu nationalist movement known as the Inkatha Freedom Party to counter the ANC, which increased the violence, but Mandela requested a meeting with Botha, which was denied, although he secretly met with Justice Minister Kobie Coetsee in 1987, the first of eleven meetings over the next three years. Coetsee himself organized negotiations between Mandela and a governmental representation of four personalities starting in 1988; this representation accepted the release of political prisoners and the legalization of the ANC on the condition that they renounce violence, distance themselves from the South African Communist Party and cease proposing the establishment of majority rule. Mandela refused these conditions, and insisted that the ANC would end the armed struggle if the government renounced violence against the population.

But in late 1987 and early 1988 something unexpected happened on the Namibian border. FAPLA and USSR forces launched Operation Hail October in order to corner the UNITA of Jonas Savimbi, an ally of South Africa and the United States in southern Angola. The South African high command realized the danger of its ally and, for that reason, its border with Namibia, the passage of the members of the Spear of the Nation and SWAPO towards Namibian localities administered by Pretoria. To avoid this, it intervened directly in the conflict to exterminate several of the best and most armed units of the FAPLA. But they were finally defeated by Cuba. Due to the blockade, Pretoria could not modernize its army and ran the risk of not being able to defend its territory.[note 1] In the words of Robert Ross (2006, p. 195) South Africa had lost the foreign war. In order to get help from Western nations it had to show signs of fixing its problem with racism and one such sign was the treatment of Nelson Mandela.

Mandela's 70th birthday attracted international attention. Particularly noteworthy was the *Nelson Mandela 70th birthday tribute* concert held at Wembley Stadium in London, but although he was regarded as a hero around the world, personal problems arose again when ANC leaders informed him that Winnie had become the head of a criminal gang known as the "Mandela United Football Club", responsible for torturing and killing opponents - including children- in Soweto. Although there were those who recommended divorce, he decided to keep the marriage until she was judicially declared guilty.

In Victor Verster's prison and release

After recovering from an attack of tuberculosis aggravated by the dampness of his cell, Mandela was transferred to the Victor Verster prison near Paarl in December 1988, where he lived with the comforts of a security guard, with a cook at his service and time to complete his studies. There he lived with the comforts of a security guard, as he had a cook at his service and had time to complete his studies. He was also allowed to receive visitors, such as anti-apartheid activist and old acquaintance Harry Schwarz. He also had secret communication with Oliver Tambo, who was in exile.By 1989 Botha suffered a stroke, and although he retained the presidency of the country, he decided to retire as the leader of the National Party and was replaced by Frederik de Klerk. In the meantime, Botha surprisingly invited Mandela to a meeting in July for tea, which Mandela himself considered a formidable gesture. Botha was replaced as president by de Klerk six weeks later. The new president believed that apartheid was unsustainable, so he unconditionally released all ANC prisoners except Mandela. With the fall of the Berlin Wall in November 1989, De Klerk convened his cabinet for a debate to discuss the legalization of the ANC, and the subsequent release of Mandela. Although the plan was strongly opposed by some, De Klerk met with Mandela in December to discuss the political situation, a meeting they both found very amicable and which was the prelude to his unconditional release from prison, along with the legalization of the underground political parties on February 2, 1990. Soon after, Mandela's photographs were allowed to be published in the country's media for the first time in twenty years.

Leaving Victor Verster Prison on February 11, Mandela held Winnie's hand in front of crowds and the press. The event was broadcast worldwide, and he was then carried through the crowds to Cape Town City Hall, where he gave a speech in which he declared his commitment to peace and reconciliation with the white minority, although he made it clear that the ANC's armed struggle was not over and would continue as a "form of defensive action against apartheid violence. He also expressed his hope that the government would enter into negotiations, "to end the armed conflict once and for all", and insisted that his main objective was to bring peace to the majority black population and give them the right to vote in general and local elections.In the following days, while living in the Desmond Tutu home, he met with friends, activists and the press, as well as making another speech to 100,000 people at Soccer City Stadium in Johannesburg.

End of apartheid

Mandela made a trip across Africa, meeting with supporters and politicians in Zambia, Zimbabwe, Namibia, Libya and Algeria, continuing to Sweden where he met with Oliver Tambo, and then on to London where he attended the *Nelson Mandela: International Tribute for a Free South Africa* concert at Wembley Stadium.On that journey, he urged governments to support sanctions against the pro-apartheid government: in France he was received by President François Mitterrand; in Vatican City by Pope John Paul II; and in the United Kingdom by Margaret Thatcher. In the United States he met with President George H. W. Bush, gave speeches in both houses of Congress and visited eight cities, being enthusiastically received by the Afro-descendant community. In Cuba he visited President Fidel Castro, of whom he was a fervent admirer and whose relationship ended in friendship.He also visited President R. Venkataraman of India; President Suharto of Indonesia; Prime Minister Mahathir Mohamad of Malaysia; Prime Minister Bob Hawke of Australia, and also visited Japan; he did not manage to visit the Soviet Union, a state that had historically supported the ANC.

In May 1990, he led a multiracial ANC delegation to begin negotiations with the government delegation of eleven Afrikaners. In the meetings, Mandela distinguished himself by his knowledge of Afrikaner history, and the talks resulted in the Groot Schuur Act, in which the government lifted the state of emergency. In August, Mandela - recognizing the ANC's military disadvantage - offered a ceasefire in the Pretoria Act, which was heavily criticized by MK members. In fact, it took him a long time to try to unify and rebuild the ANC, so he was seen at assemblies such as the Johannesburg Conference attended by 1600 people, many of whom found him to be more moderate than expected.At the ANC's July 1991 national conference in Durban, Mandela admitted the organization's mistakes and announced that his goal was to build a "strong and efficient organization" to make majority rule a reality in the country. At that conference he was elected as ANC president to replace Tambo, and an executive council composed of fifty personalities of different races was adopted.

Mandela was assigned an office in the ANC's new facilities at the Lutuli residence in downtown Johannesburg, and moved with Winnie to a large house in Soweto, where their marital relationship was strained when he learned of Winnie's extramarital affair with Dali Mpofu, although he supported her in her trial for kidnapping and assault. On the other hand, he obtained financial support for Winnie's legal defense through the International Aid Fund for South Africa and the Libyan leader Muammar Gaddafi; but in June 1991 she was convicted and sentenced to six years in prison, a sentence that was reduced to two years after an appeal. On April 13, 1992 Mandela announced his separation from Winnie. The ANC itself forced her to resign from the national council for misappropriating funds; following these incidents, Mandela moved to the Johannesburg suburb of Houghton, inhabited mostly by white neighbors. However, his reputation was tarnished by increased violence among his own people, specifically between ANC members and Inkatha supporters in KwaZulu-Natal province, in which thousands died. In response, he met with Inkatha leader Mangosuthu Buthelezi, but the ANC prevented him from continuing the talks. In fact, Mandela recognized the existence of a "third force" in South Africa that the country's intelligence service supported to increase the "killing among the population" and accused De Klerk -whom he distrusted more than ever- for the Sebokeng massacre. By September 1991, a peace conference was held in Johannesburg in which Mandela, Buthelezi and De Klerk signed a peace agreement, although the violence continued.

CODESA

The Convention for a Democratic South Africa (CODESA) opened in December 1991 at the World Trade Center in Johannesburg, attended by 228 delegates from 19 political parties. Although Cyril Ramaphosa led the ANC delegation, Mandela remained the leading figure, and after De Klerk used the final speech to condemn ANC violence, he too denounced De Klerk as the "ringleader of an illegitimate and discredited regime". Few agreements were reached at that meeting dominated by National Party and ANC supporters. A second convention (CODESA 2) was held in May 1992, where De Klerk insisted that a post-apartheid South Africa should be installed under a federal system with a rotating presidency to ensure the protection of ethnic minorities; Mandela opposed this proposal, and demanded a unitary state ruled by the majority.Following the Boipatong massacre in which ANC activists were killed by Inkatha militants with government support, Mandela ended negotiations, before attending a meeting of the Organization of African Unity in Senegal, where he convened a session of the UN Security Council at which he proposed that a peacekeeping force be deployed in South Africa to prevent "state terrorism." The United Nations delegated special envoy Cyrus Vance to South Africa to assist in the negotiations, but the ANC called for a large mobilization in August that ended in the largest strike in South African history, with a march in Pretoria.

After the Bhisho massacre, in which 28 ANC supporters and one soldier were shot dead by the Ciskei Defense Force in the midst of a march, Mandela realized that mobilizations provoked more violence, and resumed negotiations in September. He agreed to do so on the condition that all political prisoners be released; that traditional Zulu weapons be banned; and that Zulu workers' hostels be placed under surveillance. These last two demands were intended to prevent further attacks by

Inkatha. Under pressure, De Klerk agreed. In the negotiation, it was agreed that a general election including all ethnic groups would be held, resulting in a coalition government and a Constitutional Assembly that would ensure that the National Party would maintain its influence in South African politics. For its part, the ANC pledged to respect the seats of white bureaucrats. These concessions provoked much criticism within the organization. Both also agreed to the proclamation of an interim constitution that would guarantee the separation of powers, the creation of a constitutional court and the inclusion of a Bill of Rights as in the United States; likewise, the country was divided into nine provinces, each governed by a premier who would have his respective civil service, which pleased both De Klerk's desire for federalism and Mandela's desire for a unitary government.

The democratic process was threatened by the Compromised South African Group (COSAG), an alliance of far-right Afrikaners and black secessionists belonging to Inkatha, and in June 1993 the white supremacist Afrikaner Weerstandsbeweging (AWB) attacked the World Trade Center in Kempton Park, a suburb of Johannesburg.Following the assassination of ANC leader Chris Hani, Mandela made a public speech to calm any attempted uprising and later appeared at the mass funeral of Oliver Tambo in Soweto, who had died of a stroke.In July 1993, both Mandela and De Klerk visited the United States and held separate meetings with Bill Clinton at which each received the Presidential Medal of Freedom.Subsequently, they were awarded the Nobel Peace Prize in Norway.

Mandela, under the influence of the young ANC leader Thabo Mbeki, also held meetings with business personalities and began to dispense with his interest in any nationalization policy, which could alienate international investors of such importance to the country in those years.

Although he was criticized by socialist-leaning ANC members, he received support for promoting private enterprise from the Chinese and Vietnamese communist parties in January 1992 at the World Economic Forum in Switzerland, and made a short appearance as a schoolteacher reciting a speech by Malcolm X in the final scene of the film of the same name.

The 1994 general elections

With general elections scheduled for April 27, 1994, the ANC launched its own campaign, opening 100 election offices and hiring consultant Stanley Greenberg. Greenberg organized the popular forums around the country, at which Mandela made his presence felt. By then he was already a very popular and respected personality among black South Africans, and the ANC promoted the Reconstruction and Development Program, which aimed to build one million houses in five years, establish universal education, and provide access to water and electricity services. The party's slogan was "A better life for all", although it did not explain in detail how these proposals would be carried out. With the exception of the *Weekly Mail* and *New Nation* newspapers, the South African press was generally opposed to Mandela's victory in the elections, as they feared permanent ethnic conflicts, and therefore supported the Democratic Party.Mandela also made efforts to seek financial support for the ANC, traveling to North America, Europe and Asia to meet with potential donors, including those who had supported apartheid. He also demanded a reduction in the minimum voting age, a proposal rejected by the ANC and which ended up being the object of ridicule.

Concerned about any attempt by COSAG to sabotage the elections, and prior to the failed Bofutatsuana coup and Shell House massacre executed by the AWB and Inkatha respectively, Mandela met with senior Afrikaner politicians and military officers, including Pieter Willem Botha, Pik Botha and Constand Viljoen. He strove to make himself credible so that everyone would work within a democratic system, and he enlisted De Klerk's help in convincing Inkatha members to participate in the elections, rather than launch a war of secession. Moreover, as leaders of the major political parties, De Klerk and Mandela appeared in a television debate. Although De Klerk was considered the better speaker, Mandela's gesture of shaking his hand surprised him, and analysts saw it as a personal triumph.

The elections were conducted with few outbreaks of violence, although a faction of the AWB detonated several car bombs that killed 20 people. As expected, the ANC won by a landslide, claiming 62% of the vote, close to the two-thirds required to unilaterally change the constitution. In fact, the ANC won in seven provinces, with the remaining two going to the National Party and Inkatha. Mandela cast his vote at Ohlange High School in the city of Durban, and although the ANC victory made him president of the republic, he accepted in public that the elections had been marred by attempts at fraud and sabotage.

Chair

The first political act of the new National Assembly was the election of Mandela as the first black president in South Africa's history. The inauguration took place in Pretoria on May 9, 1994, and was broadcast to one billion television viewers worldwide, with 4,000 guests in attendance, including world leaders from a variety of backgrounds. The event was attended by 4,000 guests, including world leaders from different backgrounds. Mandela headed an ANC-dominated Government of National Unity, with no experience in governmental decision-making, and was accompanied by representatives of the National Party and Inkatha. Under the interim constitution, these two parties took no fewer than 20 seats; and in accordance with earlier negotiations, De Klerk became vice president and Thabo Mbeki the second vice president. Although Mbeki had not been his first choice for the post, Mandela increased his confidence in him as the presidency wore on, thus allowing him to arrange for the organization of certain state policies.Mandela moved to his presidential office in Tuynhuys, Cape Town, and allowed De Klerk to reside at Groote Schuur instead of staying at the nearby Westbrook mansion, which the president renamed "Genadendal," meaning "valley of mercy" in the Afrikaans language.The new ruler kept his house in Houghton and had one built in Qunu, which he visited regularly, taking the opportunity to walk in the surrounding area, meet with neighbors and settle tribal disputes.

At 76 Mandela was suffering from various ailments, and although he took great pains to appear healthy to the public, he felt isolated and lonely, yet he rubbed shoulders with world entertainment figures such as Michael Jackson, Whoopi Goldberg and the Spice Girls, as well as eminent business and political personalities such as Harry Oppenheimer of Anglo-American, and Queen Elizabeth II who visited South Africa in March 1995, earning him much criticism from anti-capitalist ANC members.Although he was surrounded by comforts, Mandela's routine life was simple, and he donated his annual income of R552 000 to the Nelson Mandela Children's Fund, which he had founded in 1995. On the other hand, although he supported freedom of the press and was a friend of many journalists, he was very critical of the South African media. Apart from pointing out that most of them were owned by middle-class businessmen, all of them white, he reproached them for the disproportionate way in which they highlighted the country's crimes, without delving into the reality of the facts.

As for his intimacy, Mandela changed his clothes several times a day, but he was particularly known for wearing the Batik-designed shirts popularly called "Madiba shirts", which he wore even at official ceremonies.By December 1994 his autobiography *A Long Walk to Freedom* was published;and he also attended the 49th ANC conference in Bloemfontein at which a more radical national council in its political stance had been elected. There was Winnie Mandela who - in connection with her marriage to Nelson - had expressed an interest in reconciliation. By contrast, he would initiate divorce proceedings in August 1995. In fact, by that time he was in a relationship with Mozambican Graça Machel, a 50-year-old political activist and widow of former President Samora Machel. They had met in July 1999 when she was in mourning, but the friendship had strengthened to the point that she accompanied Mandela on several official visits abroad. Graça had turned down Nelson's first marriage proposal, as she wanted time for her work in both Mozambique and Johannesburg.

National reconciliation

For Mandela, national reconciliation was his main objective in his presidency, as the protagonist of the transition from a country ruled by a minority under apartheid policies to a democratic and multicultural nation.He was aware of the economic ruin of other African countries that had been abandoned by white minorities in the post-colonial years, so he made sure that the white South African population was protected and felt part of the *Rainbow Nation*. He therefore took it upon himself to create a coalition in his cabinet as heterogeneous as possible, with De Klerk as his deputy president. Other important National Party supporters filled important posts for the ministries of Agriculture, Energy, Environment and Minerals and Energy; while Buthelezi was appointed to the post of Minister of Internal Affairs.The other cabinet posts were given to ANC members, many of whom - such as Joe Modise, Alfred Nzo, Joe Slovo, Mac Maharaj and Dullah Omar - had known each other for many years, although others - such as Tito Mboweni and Jeff Radebe - were younger. However, Mandela's relationship with De Klerk had been strained, as the president felt that De Klerk had provocative attitudes, and De Klerk felt that he was humiliated by the president. For instance, in January 1995 Mandela reprimanded him for having granted amnesty to 3500 policemen before the general elections, and later criticized him for having defended former defense minister Magnus Malan when he was accused of murder.

Mandela personally met with well-known figures of the apartheid regime, among them Betsie Schoombie, widow of Hendrik Verwoerd, as well as the lawyer Percy Yutar, and during his government he emphasized forgiveness and reconciliation, since, as he said, "the brave are not afraid of forgiveness if it helps to foster peace. During his government he emphasized forgiveness and reconciliation, because, he said, "the brave are not afraid of forgiveness, if it helps to foster peace. He also encouraged black South Africans to leave behind their hatred of the national rugby team, the *Springboks*, when South Africa hosted the 1995 World Cup. After the final, won by South Africa over New Zealand, Mandela presented the trophy to captain Francois Pienaar wearing the *Springbok* jersey with the number 6 on the back, which belonged to Pienaar himself. This gesture was recognized as a major step towards reconciliation between black and white South Africans. As De Klerk put it: "Mandela won the hearts of millions of white rugby fans. Mandela's constant striving for national reconciliation dispelled the fears of white citizens, but it also brought him criticism from the more radical black political militants. In fact, his wife Winnie accused the ANC of being interested in seeking to win the will of *whites* rather than helping *blacks*.

Mandela also verified the formation of the Truth and Reconciliation Commission to investigate crimes committed during the apartheid regime by both the government and the ANC, and commissioned Desmond Tutu as its chairman. To avoid exalting martyrs, the commission granted amnesty in exchange for testimonies of crimes committed during those years. The work began in February 1996 and took two years of taking testimonies of rape, torture, bombings and assassinations before the final report was released in October 1998. Both De Klerk and Mbeki requested that some parts of the report be deleted, but only De Klerk's request was granted. Mandela congratulated the commission for its work, saying it had "helped to put the past behind us and concentrate on the present and the future.

Government

Mandela's government inherited a country with economic inequality and a public service that functioned very differently in communities where it depended on whether the population was majority white or black. With a population of 40 million, some 23 million had no electricity or public health services; 12 million had no clean water; and two million children did not attend school in a society where one-third of the population was illiterate. There was 33% unemployment, and just under half lived below the poverty line. State funds were on the verge of bankruptcy, with 5% of the budget spent on debt repayment, causing the promises of the Reconstruction and Development Program to be delayed, so there was no prospect of realizing nationalization or job creation policies. However, the government adopted liberal economic policies to promote foreign investment, in line with the Washington Consensus recommended by the World Bank and the International Monetary Fund.

During Mandela's presidency, the social protection policy was increased to 13% in 1996/97 and maintained in 1997/98, although it was lowered to 7% in 1998/99. However, the government introduced equal benefits for communities, including people with disabilities, child support and pensions for the elderly, which had been provided on the basis of racial groups prior to his administration.By 1994, free medical care was established for children under six and pregnant women, a policy that was extended in 1996 to all those requiring primary health care.By the 1999 elections, the ANC could boast that - due to its policies - some three million people had managed to obtain telephone lines; 1.5 million children had enrolled in the education system; 500 clinics had been rebuilt; two million people had benefited from electricity service; access to water service had been extended to three million people; and 750,000 houses had been built to house three million inhabitants.

With the backing of the 1994 Land Restitution Law, people who had lost their property - as a result of the Native Land Law of 1913 - were allowed to make their respective claims, which led to the admission of close to 10,000 petitions.Counteracting the negative effects of the land law issued in 1913 that guaranteed the dominion of 87% of the Union territory for the white minority, the Property Reform Law no. 3 of 1996 secured the rights of land holders who lived, cultivated or raised livestock on farms. With this legislation, such holders were protected from being evicted without a court order, and those who were over 65 years of age. Other legal tools were the Workers' Skills Development Act of 1998, which established mechanisms to fund skills and abilities in any workplace.The Labor Relations Act of 1995 promoted workplace democracy, collective bargaining, and labor dispute resolution; the Minimum Conditions of Employment Act of 1997 improved the protection of workers' basic rights; and the Equal Employment Act of 1998 was passed to prevent discrimination and ensure its enforcement in the workplace.

Edwin Cameron accused Mandela of having done little to counteract the AIDS pandemic; by 1999, 10% of South Africans were HIV positive, and Mandela himself admitted he had been negligent, leaving the problem in the hands of Thabo Mbeki. Mandela himself admitted that he had been negligent and left the problem in the hands of Thabo Mbeki. He was also criticized for the increase in crime, as South Africa had one of the highest crime rates; this was the main cause of the emigration of 7,500,000 white people at the end of the 1990s. Similarly, during his administration there were corruption scandals, and he was accused of having failed to counteract this problem.

International relations

Taking South Africa itself as a model, Mandela urged other countries to resolve their conflicts through diplomacy and reconciliation. He echoed Mbeki's words for an "African renaissance", and was very concerned about all the problems of the continent; in fact, he made diplomatic moves to overthrow the military junta of Sani Abacha in Nigeria, and later became a protagonist for his regime to be sanctioned for increasing violations of human rights.In 1996 he was elected to the post of president of the Southern African Development Community and initiated negotiations to end the First Congo War in Zaire, which, however, were unsuccessful. In South Africa's first post-apartheid military action in Lesotho, the president ordered the deployment of troops in that country in September 1998 to protect the government of Prime Minister Pakalitha Mosisili after a disputed election that provoked popular uprisings.

That same September, he was elected as secretary general of the Non-Aligned Movement, which held its annual conference in Durban. At that event he criticized the "chauvinistic and timorous interests" of the Israeli government that had stalled negotiations to end the Israeli-Palestinian conflict, and urged India and Pakistan to negotiate an end to the Kashmir conflict, for which he received criticism from both Israel and India. On the other hand, and due to the economic prosperity of the East Asian countries, he tried to promote trade relations with Malaysia, despite the fact that this country had fallen into the 1997 Asian financial crisis.

He was also responsible for intervening in the dispute between Libya and the U.S.-British alliance in the trial of two Libyan nationals (Abdelbaset al-Megrahi and Lamin Khalifah Fhimah) who had been indicted in November

1991 for the bombing of Pan Am Flight 103. Mandela proposed that they be tried in a third state, which was agreed to by the parties. Under Scottish law, the trial was held at Camp Zeist in the Netherlands in April 1999, and one of them was found guilty.

In fact, he caused much controversy because of his relationship with Indonesian President Suharto, whose regime had been responsible for human rights abuses, although in private meetings he urged him to withdraw from East Timor.

He also came in for a lot of criticism from Western countries because of his friendship with Fidel Castro and Muammar Gaddafi, and Castro visited him in 1998, while Mandela met Gaddafi in Libya to give him the Order of Good Hope. Castro visited him in 1998, while Mandela met Gaddafi in Libya to award him the Order of Good Hope. Upon learning of the criticism from Western countries and media, he rejected it on the grounds that it had racist undertones.

Retirement from politics

The final text of South Africa's new constitution was agreed by parliament in May 1996, and it instituted mechanisms to control all political and administrative bodies within the framework of a constitutional democracy. De Klerk, however, opposed the adoption of this fundamental law and withdrew from the governing coalition in protest, resulting in the ANC taking over the National Party's seats, while Mbeki became the country's sole deputy president. This resulted in the ANC taking over the seats of the National Party, while Mbeki became the country's sole deputy president. When Mandela and Mbeki were absent from South Africa on one occasion, Buthelezi was appointed acting president, which improved the relationship with Mandela.

Mandela resigned as ANC president at the 1997 party conference, and although he expected Cyril Ramaphosa to replace him, the ANC elected Mbeki to the post, which for Mandela meant that Mbeki had become the *de facto* president of South Africa. To replace Mbeki as deputy president, Mandela and the executive council supported the candidacy of Jacob Zuma, of Zulu origin, who had been imprisoned on Robben Island. Although Winnie Mandela claimed to be the opposition candidate, as her populist rhetoric had won her many supporters, Zuma defeated her by a significant margin in the respective election.

On the other hand, the sentimental relationship between Mandela and Graça Machel was thriving, so that in February 1998 the president stated in public that "he was in love with a great lady" and - pressured by his friend Desmond Tutu who insisted that he set an example for the youth - arranged for the marriage to take place on his 80th birthday.

South Africa's 1996 constitution prevented the president of the country from serving two consecutive terms. Mandela did not attempt to amend this article; in fact, it was never in his interest to do so. He therefore gave his farewell speech on March 29, 1999, which was followed by his retirement from public life.

After retirement

Upon retiring from political life in June 1999, Mandela wanted a quiet life with his family, so he divided his time between Johannesburg and Qunu. He also began the sequel to his first autobiography, which was to be titled *The Years in the Presidency*, but the idea was abandoned before publication.However, the isolation became uncomfortable for him, so he returned to public activity which still offered him many occupations, such as meetings with world leaders and celebrities; and while in Johannesburg he worked with the Nelson Mandela Foundation which was founded in 1999 for rural development, building schools and combating Aids.Although he had received much criticism for his poor work to counteract the AIDS pandemic during his presidency, he dedicated himself to it after his retirement and described the dire situation as a "war" that had killed more victims than all "wars in the past", and urged the Mbeki government to ensure that South Africans suffering from AIDS had access to antiretrovirals.In 2000, the *Nelson Mandela Invitational* golf tournament was founded to raise funds for charity, hosted by Gary Player, and in July 2001, Mandela was treated for prostate cancer with favorable results.

In 2002 he inaugurated the Nelson Mandela Annual Lecture, and in 2003 he created the Mandela Rhodes Foundation at Rhodes House, Oxford University, to provide university scholarships to African students. Other subsequent projects included the Nelson Mandela Remembrance Center and the *46664* concert series to raise funds for AIDS. Other activities included the closing speech at the 13th International AIDS Conference in Durban in 2000, and again in 2004 at the same conference in Bangkok, Thailand.

On the other hand, Mandela increased his criticism of the policies of Western nations. He opposed the 1999 NATO intervention in Kosovo, which he called an attempt by the most powerful nations to become "policemen" of the world.In 2003 he spoke out against U.S.-U.K. plans to launch the Iraq War, which he described as a "tragedy," and sharply criticized President George W. Bush and British Prime Minister Tony Blair for undermining the role of the United Nations. In fact, he stated that "All he (Mr. Bush) wanted was Iraqi oil" and declared that the U.S. government had committed more "atrocities" around the globe than any other nation, and brought up the atomic bombs in Japan in World War II. These words provoked much controversy internationally, although he ended up reconciling particularly with Blair.He also maintained his interest in relations between Libya and the UK, so he visited Abdelbaset al-Megrahi in Barlinnie prison and took a stand against the conditions in which he was being held, which he called "psychological intimidation".

Last years

In June 2004, at the age of 85 and in poor health, Mandela announced his definitive retirement from public life with these words: "Don't call me, I will call you". Although he continued to meet with friends and his own family, the Foundation ruled out any public appearances on his behalf and denied requests for interviews.

However, he still wielded some influence in international politics. In 2005 he founded the Nelson Mandela Legacy Trust during a trip to the United States, where he spoke at the Brookings Institution and the NAACP to raise funds for the African continent. He also held meetings with Senator Hillary Clinton and President George W. Bush and for the first time greeted then Senator Barack Obama. He also urged Zimbabwean President Robert Mugabe to step down in view of increasing human rights violations in that country. When that failed, he spoke out against Mugabe in 2007, urging him to step down with "whatever respect and dignity he had left". That same year, Mandela, Machel and Desmond Tutu brought world leaders together in Johannesburg to contribute their wisdom and leadership to solving the world's most pressing problems. Together with them, he gave birth to the group The Elders during a speech on the occasion of his 89th birthday.

Mandela's 90th birthday was celebrated across the country, mainly in Qunu, and a concert was held in his honor in Hyde Park, London. During a speech for the occasion, he urged the world's millionaires to help the underprivileged. Even during Thabo Mbeki's presidency, he continued to support the ANC, although he was overshadowed by Mbeki himself at the events they both attended. In fact, Mandela was more familiar with Jacob Zuma, although the Foundation was upset when his grandson, Mandla Mandela, flew him to the Eastern Cape in 2009 for an event in support of Zuma in the middle of a storm.

In 2004, he spearheaded a successful campaign for South Africa to host the 2010 World Cup, stressing that it would be an "ideal gift" for the country since the end of apartheid. Although he kept a low profile during the event due to his ill health, he made his last appearance at the closing ceremony where he received a warm welcome. That year, Nelson Mandela was awarded an honorary doctorate by six universities in the Laureate International Universities network. On May 7, 2010, in the city of Madrid, the then South African ambassador to Spain received the award on Mandela's behalf.

In February 2011, he was briefly hospitalized due to a respiratory infection, which attracted international attention.In December 2012, he was again admitted to the hospital for a lung infection, as well as the removal of gallstones.After a successful operation in March 2013,the lung infection reappeared, so he was again hospitalized in Pretoria for a few days.Until that date, and since 2005, his relatives had been engaged in legal disputes regarding the burial place of both the children and Mandela himself.On June 8, 2013, the infection complicated the burial place of the children and Mandela himself.Until that date, and since 2005, his relatives had been engaged in legal disputes regarding the burial place of both the children and Mandela himself.On June 8, 2013, the infection became more complicated, and he was hospitalized in serious condition.After four days, it was made known that his condition was serious although he remained stable.It was also made known that the ambulance that had transported him had broken down en route, leaving him on the street for 40 minutes. The government was criticized for this incident, but Zuma assured that the former president was under the best medical care.

On June 22, 2013, CBS News announced that Mandela had not opened his eyes in several days, was unresponsive to stimuli, and that the family was discussing the best medical care for the patient at this critical time. His former bodyguard, Shaun van Heerden, who was introduced by the BBC as "Mandela's closest companion for the past 12 years," publicly urged the family to "leave him alone" a week earlier. On June 23, Zuma announced that Mandela's condition had become critical. Zuma, accompanied by ANC Deputy President Cyril Ramaphosa, visited Graça Machel in Pretoria hospital and discussed his condition. By June 25, Archbishop Thabo Makgoba visited and prayed with Machel at "that very hard time of observation and expectation." The following day, Zuma revisited Mandela in the hospital and canceled a scheduled appointment in Mozambique, and a relative of Mandela's told *The Daily Telegraph* that the former president was on advanced life support.

By July 4, news circulated that David Smith, Mandela's family lawyer, had testified in court that the former president was in a vegetative state and that advanced life support should be withdrawn; however, the presidential offices stated that the doctors treating Mandela had denied that he was in a vegetative state. By July 10, it was reported from the presidency that Mandela was in critical but stable condition and was responding to treatment. By September 1, he was removed from the hospital, although his condition was unstable.

Death and funeral

After suffering from a prolonged respiratory infection, Nelson Mandela died on December 5, 2013 at the age of 95. He passed away at around 20:50 South African time (UTC+2) at his home in Houghton, Johannesburg, surrounded by his family.His death was announced by South African President Jacob Zuma on television.

On December 6, Zuma declared national mourning for a period of ten days, and announced that the funeral would be held at Soccer City Stadium in Johannesburg on the 10th of the same month. He also declared December 8 as the National Day of Prayer and Reflection. Mandela's remains were displayed between December 11 and 13 at Union Buildings in Pretoria while the state funeral was held on December 15 in Qunu, with an estimated 90 representatives from various countries traveling to South Africa for the funeral ceremonies.

Mandela's estate, estimated at US$4.1 million, was divided among his widow, family members, employees and educational institutions.

Political ideology

Mandela was a supporter of African nationalism, of which he was a believer since he was part of the ANC,and he also considered himself a social democrat.He therefore declared himself opposed "to capitalism, private ownership of land and the power of billionaires".He was influenced by Marxism and was an advocate of scientific socialism.During the *Treason Trial* he denied being a communist.

Although years later historians and biographers asserted that this had been a lie. In fact, biographer David Jones claimed that Mandela was "a supporter of communism and communists" in the late 1950s and early 1960s, while historian Stephen Ellis found evidence that he had been an active member of the SACP. This was confirmed after his death by the SACP itself and the ANC. According to the SACP, he had not only been a member of the party, but had been part of its central committee when he was arrested in 1962 despite his political denials.Despite all this, he himself in his autobiography and various interviews denied his affinity for Marxism.

The 1955 Freedom Charter, which Mandela participated in drafting, called for the nationalization of banking, gold mining and land, as it was believed necessary to ensure the distribution of wealth.Despite these positions, Mandela did not carry out any nationalization during his presidency, as he feared that foreign investors would withdraw from the country.[*citation needed*]

This decision was influenced in part by the collapse of the socialist states of the Soviet Union and the Eastern European bloc in the early 1990's. Although he presented himself as an "autocrat" in his speeches, he was a guarantor of democracy who supported the decision of the majorities even though he did not share many of their decisions.He held the conviction that "inclusiveness, stability and freedom of speech" were the foundations of democracy, and was a believer in natural law and human rights. These principles led him not only to seek race equality, but also to promote gay rights as part of the post-apartheid reforms.

Private life

Mandela was a very private person who hid his emotions and trusted very few people. He lived an austere life and shunned alcohol and tobacco. He had the peculiarity of making his own bed, even when he held the office of president, and was known for his sense of humor.There were those who considered him to be a stubborn man who occasionally lost his temper, although he was recognized as a loyal man.He was usually friendly and cordial, and was relaxed in conversation, even in the face of his opponents.Polite and courteous, he was also very helpful to anyone, regardless of age or social status, and also chatted with children and domestic help.As an older man he appreciated the good qualities of people, even if he had to defend his detractors to his own allies, who themselves thought he was too trusting.He was very concerned about his image and over the years always looked for the best clothes, which led many to think he had an air of royalty about him.His personal biographer Anthony Sampson commented that he was a "master of image and demeanor," which caused him to present himself in the best light at photo shoots and to deliver quotes appropriate to the occasion.Describing his own life, Mandela said he was "not a Messiah, but an ordinary man who became a leader through extraordinary circumstances."

He married three times, fathered six children, and had 17 grandchildren and 16 great-grandchildren at the time of his death. He was usually serious and demanding with his own children, although he was more affectionate with his great-grandchildren.His first marriage to Evelyn Mase took place in October 1944; they divorced 13 years later in 1957 amidst crippling accusations of adultery, estrangement from home for his work, a commitment to political activity and Evelyn's adherence to the Jehovah's Witnesses, a religion that required her to be politically neutral.The couple procreated two sons who died before

Mandela: Madiba *Thembi* Thembekile (1945-1969) and Makgatho Mandela (1950-2005); the former died in a traffic accident and the latter of AIDS. They also had two daughters, both named Makaziwe Mandela (born in 1947 and 1954 respectively); the first died at nine months of age and the second, known as *Maki*, survived Mandela. Makgatho's son, Mandla Mandela, was head of the Mvezo tribal council in 2007.

His second wife, Winnie Mandela, also hailed from the Transkei area, although the two met in Johannesburg where she became the first black social worker. The two had two daughters, both diplomats, Zenani Mandela-Dlamini, born on February 4, 1959, and Zindziswa Mandela-Hlongwane, Zindzi Mandela, born in 1960. Zindzi was 18 months old when her father was sent to Robben Island. Winnie was later marred by family disputes that reflected the country's troubled political situation; in fact, separation (in April 1992) and divorce (in March 1996) were marred by the political discord of those years.Mandela's third wife was Graça Machel (born Simbine), whom he married on his 80th birthday in 1998.

Influence and legacy

At the time of his death, Nelson Mandela was considered the "father of the South African nation", as well as the "founding father of democracy", and the "emancipator of the nation, its savior, its George Washington and its Abraham Lincoln".Mandela's biographer, Anthony Sampson, stated that even during his lifetime the myth had developed around his person, and was "so strong, it blurred reality", which made him a kind of "secular saint".Mandela's presidency, after a decade, has been regarded as "the golden years of hope and social harmony", and outside South Africa he gained worldwide respect for his activism against apartheid and for promoting reconciliation between the different races, and has been valued as a "moral authority" who had a "zeal for truth".

Throughout his life he was also the target of criticism. Margaret Thatcher described the ANC as a "typical terrorist organization" in 1987, which drew the attention of international opinion, although she later urged Botha to release Mandela.upon his death, countless Twitter users retorted allegations that Mandela had been a communist and terrorist, while anti-abortion activists around the world took the occasion to speak out against him for having supported the Free Abortion Act in 1996.He was also criticized for his friendship with political leaders such as Fidel Castro, Muammar Gaddafi, Akbar Hashemi Rafsanjani and Suharto, as well as his refusal to condemn the human rights violations of which they are accused.

Orders, decorations and monuments

On December 16, 2013, South Africa's Day of Reconciliation, a 9-meter tall bronze statue was unveiled at Union Buildings by President Jacob Zuma. In 2004 the municipality of Johannesburg awarded him the *Keys to the City*, and the Sandton Square shopping center was renamed Nelson Mandela Square, after a statue was erected there.By 2008 another statue was installed at the Drakenstein Correctional Centre, formerly known as Victor Verster Prison, near Cape Town, right on the site where Mandela was released.

In 1991 the Complutense University of Madrid awarded him an honorary doctorate. In 1992 he received the Prince of Asturias Award for International Cooperation, and in 1993 he received the Nobel Peace Prize together with Frederik de Klerk. In November 2009, the United Nations Assembly proclaimed his birthday, July 18, as "Nelson Mandela International Day" for his contribution to the fight against apartheid. On that day, the population is urged to do something for the benefit of others for 67 minutes, the same number of years that the president was part of the movement.

He was awarded the Presidential Medal of Freedom and an honorary citation of the Order of Canada, and was the first living person to receive an honorary citizenship of the same nation.Mandela was the last person to receive the Lenin Peace Prize and the first to receive the Gaddafi International Human Rights Award.In 1990, he received the Bharat Ratna Award from the Government of India and in 1992 he received the Order of Pakistan. That same year he was awarded the Atatürk International Peace Prize, which he rejected at first because he alleged the violation of human rights committed in Turkey in those years, although he later accepted it in 1999.In 1997, he was awarded the World Peace & Liberty Award by the World Jurist Association at the Cape Town conference, which has also been received by René Cassin, Sir Winston Churchill, King Philip VI and Ruth Bader Ginsburg.In 1999 he also received the Collar of the Order of Isabella the Catholic, Queen Elizabeth II made him a Bailiff Grand Cross of the Most Venerable Order of St. John (on the recommendation of the Order's Honors and Awards Committee) and he was awarded membership of the United Kingdom Order of Merit (a personal gift from the monarch).

Sports tributes

On Wednesday, May 16, 2018, FC Barcelona participated in the Mandela Centenary Cup by playing against Mamelodi Sundowns FC at the First National Bank Stadium in Johannesburg, formerly known as Soccer City Stadium. The match ended with a score of 3-1 in favor of Barça and was witnessed by the current president of FIFA; although, at the time, general secretary of UEFA, Gianni Intantino; by the former president of the United States, Barack Obama; and by the actor Leonardo Di Caprio, among others.

The match was part of the celebrations that took place in South Africa during 2018 to celebrate the centenary of Madiba's birth. This match was organized by the company RG Consultant & Sports Solutions and managed by the Tenerife businessman Rayco Garcia. This organization was supported by SAFA - the South African Football Association, LaLiga's program - LaLiga World Challenge, Mamelodi Sundowns FC, the Nelson Mandela Foundation, FC Barcelona and The Motsepe Foundation. After eleven years Barça returned to engage with the man who put an end to *apartheid* racism and violence in South Africa.

Barcelona took this match very seriously, taking its main players to what was, for Andrés Iniesta, the penultimate match in the azulgrana's colours. The Wizard of Fuentealbilla, as he is known, was also returning to the Soccer Stadium, where he gave the title to Spain, scoring a goal in the extra time of the 2010 World Cup final against the Netherlands. Coach Ernesto Valverde played with two very different lineups in this friendly and Lionel Messi participated in the last fifteen minutes of the match.

With just 2:33 on the clock, Ousmane Dembelé started the party and opened the scoring, after a mistake in the home team's defense. After 19 minutes, Luis Suárez beat goalkeeper Onyango to make the score 2-0. The final score of the match came thanks to goals from: Andre Gomes in the 66th minute, for FC Barcelona, and Memelodi Sundowns attacker Sibusiso Vilakazi in the 75th minute.

Musical tributes

Several artists have dedicated songs to Mandela. One of the most popular was "Free Nelson Mandela", recorded by The Special AKA in 1983, which was also successfully performed by Elvis Costello. Stevie Wonder dedicated the tune "I Just Called to Say I Love You" to him, winner of the 1984 Oscar Award for Best Original Song, which resulted in the censorship of his songs by the South African Broadcasting Corporation. In 1985 Youssou N'Dour's album, *Nelson Mandela*, was the first song released by the Senegalese artist in the United States. Other artists who released songs or videos honoring Mandela include Pablo Milanés, Johnny Clegg, Hugh Masekela, Brenda Fassie, Khadja Nin, Beyond, Nickelback, Raffi, and Ampie du Preez and AB de Villiers. South African singer Zahara, an ambassador for the Nelson Mandela Hospital, released the *Nelson Mandela* EP paying tribute to him. It was released when he was very ill at the Medi-Clinic hospital in Pretoria, and in the mid-1990s there was the American band The Mandela Strikeforce (translated as *The Mandela Strikeforce*) by members of Ink & Dagger.

Film and television

Mandela's life has been portrayed in film and television on several occasions. He was played by actor Danny Glover in the 1987 HBO telefilm *Mandela*. The 1997 film, *Mandela and de Klerk*, starred Sidney Poitier as the president, and Dennis Haysbert played him in *Goodbye Bafana* (2007).In the 2009 BBC television film, *Mrs Mandela*, he was played by David Harewood, as well as Morgan Freeman in the film *Invictus* (2009). Terrence Howard played the role of the president in the 2001 film, *Winnie Mandela*; and also by Idris Elba in the 2013 film, *Mandela: Long Walk to Freedom*.

*

See all our published books here:
https://campsite.bio/unitedlibrary